Trophy Terrain
Series Volume 1:
Creeks & Ditches

Bill Winke

Petersen's Bowhunting
6385 Flank Drive, Suite 800
Harrisburg, PA 17112
www.bowhuntingmag.com

Trophy Terrain Series Volume 1: Creeks & Ditches

Petersen's Bowhunting
Publisher: Jeff Waring
Editor: Christian Berg
Associate Editor: Drew Pellman
Art Director: David J. Siegfried

Unless otherwise indicated, most of the photographs in the chapters to follow were taken by the author, Bill Winke.

First Edition

Library of Congress Cataloging-in-Publication Data
ISBN (10) = 978-1-934622-46-9
ISBN (13) = 1-934622-46-X

Contents

Introduction

Ten percent of the hunters take 90 percent of the best bucks every year because those hunters focus on fundamentals.

In this world of fast food, overnight mail, instant messaging and quick fixes for everything from your broken-down marriage to your broken-down Volkswagen, many hunters are looking for a low monthly payment route to success in the deer woods. Unfortunately, it doesn't work that way. The best deer hunters spend a lot of time in the woods and earn their success over many years. There is no shortcut.

It is often said that the top 10 percent of hunters kill 90 percent of the best bucks every year. If so, I wager that they found consistent success not by using a certain product or a never-fail strategy. While every tool has its place, they have shot more than their share of nice bucks by staying focused on the fundamentals. They do the basic stuff really well.

Success truly does hinge on how well you do just a few basic things. Applying the fundamentals to the best of your ability, day after day and season after season, will produce a photo album full of deer-hunting memories. That is how you do it — no secrets, just the fundamentals — done perfectly.

In this book, I am going to focus on the fundamentals. It may not seem glamorous, but I am betting that before you are done reading it, you will agree the basics are the key. I'll also bet you'll discover you aren't focusing on them hard enough.

THE MOST IMPORTANT FUNDAMENTAL

The most important single thing you can do to shoot more bucks is to keep the element of surprise in your favor. That's it. Once the deer know you are hunting them, your chances sink faster than a big-league spitball.

If you are wondering whether you are a good deer hunter, I have one question that will help you clear that up: how often do you spook deer? Good hunters have learned to avoid detection on every level. Not only are they sticklers for where they hunt, wind direction, staying still on stand, moving at the right time and all the usual stuff, but they also know how to avoid detection when traveling to and

The best deer hunters are sticklers for every detail of the hunt. If there is a variable they can control, they will make every effort to control it. One of the key variables is doing everything possible to keep the deer from knowing they are being hunted.

Maintaining the element of surprise encompasses everything you do when hunting, from how you prepare your gear and where you hunt all the way to the fine points of choosing a spot to park your vehicle.

from their stands. They never stop thinking about ways to do it better!

When you start to look at all the different ways this simple goal of maintaining the element of surprise can affect your hunting, you will realize this thing has roots that spread in every direction like a big, old oak tree. There is just as much that you don't see as there is above the ground.

Preserving the element of surprise affects everything you do from the time you get out of bed each day until you are back home after the evening hunt. Seriously, it is part of every aspect of the hunt. What detergent to use, what type of clothing to wear, where to park, how fast to drive, how fast to walk, what time to walk to your stand, what route to take, which stand to hunt, how often to hunt your best stands, whether to rattle or grunt while on stand, when to call, how much to call, etc. The list goes on and on.

All these decisions make a big difference in the outcome of the hunt. It is a lot to manage, but that is the secret to consistency — you can't let the deer know you are hunting them. That is the most important fundamental and there is no length too great in your quest to attain this goal.

From that long list, two items stand out — which stand to hunt and what route to use to get to and from that stand. Low-impact stand sites and low-impact entry and exit routes don't often have the same mailing address. But in this book, it is my

Preserving the element of surprise is the most important thing you can do as a deer hunter. That takes many forms, but one of the most significant ones is using only low-profile entry and exit routes to your stands.

goal to help you find a way to combine the best of both. That is where this discussion of fundamentals starts to swing back to the central topic of this book — the terrain.

I am going to discuss how creeks and ditches can help you find some really productive low-impact stands and maintain the element of surprise by keeping your entry and exit route a secret from all the deer.

Usually the best stands — the ones that overlook the most sign — are hard to approach without alerting deer. When you start to understand the simple beauty of what you can do with creeks and ditches, you will see that these terrain features are perfect for whitetail hunting.

WHY TERRAIN IS SUCH A BIG PART OF DEER HUNTING

I have been fortunate enough to have lived in and hunted in some of the best whitetail country in North America. Experience has been my greatest teacher, and the number one lesson it has taught me is the value of finding something consistent and simple on which to build your strategy. It is the fundamentals again. If you focus on the stuff you know to be true, you can ignore everything else and enjoy greater simplicity and greater success.

Think of all the options a mature whitetail buck has when traveling. He may not even know himself where he is going to be next, and yet you are supposed to figure that out and put a stand up in his path? You need something to guide you

— something you can rely on. You need to play the odds. Without doing that, you might as well throw a dart at the map and hang a stand where it hits.

I have learned that a mature buck's travel patterns are often affected by something that we can easily find and understand: the terrain. Bucks relate to the terrain in a predictable way. Understanding which terrain features have the most effect on a buck's patterns, and then knowing how to find them and how to set up to hunt them, will make you a better deer hunter.

This is the first in a three-part series collectively called the Trophy Terrain Series. In each volume, we will cover a different set of terrain features and how to hunt them. Here, in Volume 1 (and in the companion DVD), I focus on helping you understand how to use the cracks and folds of the topography to achieve two primary goals: picking stand locations that will consistently produce mature buck encounters and getting to and from those locations without alerting deer.

With these two goals in mind, I now move on to the next fundamental, the important subject of entry and exit routes and why they are so important to your whitetail-hunting success.

Deer relate to the terrain as they travel. In fact, this is one of the most predictable aspects of a mature buck's behavior and one that you should understand well if you want to consistently tag them.

Deer Hunting's Real Secret

*Finding the biggest scrapes and then putting up a stand may occasionally pro-
duce action, but far too often such sign-oriented strategy is the recipe for failure.*

"Wow," the young hunter whispered as he bent over to examine the huge scrape. "I'd sure like to get a crack at the buck that made this! Maybe by dark he'll be wearing my tag." Up went the stand and right along with it the high hopes for a trophy. But alas, the only thing that came near enough to fuel the young man's scrape dreams that afternoon was a pair of squirrels.

Convinced there had to a better spot, the hunter pulled his stand and spent the next day scouting. That evening, he hunted over a big rub near a fence crossing. Nothing. The next day the hunter found a spot with "better sign," and again the results were the same — zippo. This pattern continued until the rut wound down and the season closed.

With all the sign he'd found, the hunter was perplexed when he realized he hadn't seen anything bigger than an average 8-point buck. Most of us can identify with the seemingly bad luck this hunter encountered, but none more than I, because the young hunter in the story was me back in the mid-80s. I am glad my education didn't stop with that hard lesson.

There's a whole lot more to hunting mature bucks than finding the best sign and putting up a stand. If shooting a mature buck were that easy, every hunter would have a wall full of heads. We all know that isn't the case. You have to dig a little deeper. There definitely are things known only to the most successful hunters, and once you figure out what those things are, you will gain a new satisfaction from

Low-profile entry and exit routes are the key to success. If there is a secret in deer hunting, it is the importance of micro-managing entry and exit routes so that no deer know you have passed.

deer hunting; it will all start to make sense. And you will start to kill big bucks. What I learned after a few years of beating my head against the discouragement of hunting the best sign but seeing nothing decent was the importance of how you get there and how you leave — your entry and exit routes. A stand location can never be a good one if you can't get in and out clean.

If there is a secret to hunting mature whitetails, it is related to these entry and exit routes. This is the true chess match. How you get to and from your stands determines the outcome of your season. Remember, it goes back to the most basic of fundamentals — keep the deer from knowing you are hunting them. It is much harder to do than most hunters realize.

Attention to detail is critical to achieve consistent deer-hunting success. Everything you do when hunting has an impact on your odds for success. Become a master of the details.

DETAILS, DETAILS, DETAILS

I remember talking with PSE's Pete Shepley a few years ago about great hunters he has known. He started telling me about his friend Corky Richardson, a person few other deer hunters have heard of. Pete has a lot of respect for Corky because the man is incredibly thorough in everything he does. Corky's planning is flawless and painstaking. His assessments of the options available at any point in the hunt are impressively calculated and to the moment in their timeliness. Corky is very good at breaking down the odds to determine what the animal is most likely to do next and what he needs to do as a result. In other words, he is the ultimate strategist.

Pete's friend leaves as little to chance as possible. If there is some aspect of the hunt he can control, no matter how small, he controls it. We can all learn from this kind of preparation. Every decision you make or don't make during every single day and every single minute impacts your chances for a successful season. There is no such thing as a meaningless hunt, and there is no place for lazy thinking or lazy execution.

To make this lesson more practical for a whitetail hunter, think of it this way: alerting just a single deer (A single deer? Now we are really getting down to the nitty-gritty, aren't we?) on your way to or from your stand reduces your chances for success that season. It is that simple; every little thing matters. It is all in the details.

When the bucks know you are hunting them, they become very hard to kill. The most common way they learn of your bad intentions is through sloppy entry and exit routes. They can even pick this up through the body language of other deer — the non-target deer you spooked without much care. So, if you educate one in a roundabout way, you have started the process of educating them all.

I know guys who have better track records while hunting the same farms as me. And I know guys who have worse track records. Some of that is attributable to luck, but when the same guys drag in big bucks consistently every year and other guys seem to be chasing their tails around in circles, there has to be more to it than just luck. Consistency over time is the truest test of a person's hunting strategy, and I'm always willing to learn from the guys who hang good deer every year.

Larry and Dan are two guys with whom I used to hunt. Year in and year out, Larry got into the most big bucks and Dan got into the fewest. We all hunted the same farm. We all hunted the same rut. We all showered in the same bathroom before going out (not at the same time). And we can all shoot our bows at least well enough to make clean kills out to 40 yards. On the surface, you would not

Larry Zach with a great bow kill. Larry and I hunted the same farm for nine years. While I killed some dandy bucks, Larry's bucks tended to be older and bigger most years. There is more to this than luck. Be willing to learn from hunters who are consistently successful.

Time spent thinking about and planning entry and exit routes is one aspect of preparation that separates hunters. You need to keep playing the chess match until you have figured out how to get in and out without alerting a single deer.

have seen many differences in the type of stand locations we hunted. They all overlooked reasonable buck sign.

But if you dug into the fine points of the hunt, you would have seen the gap widen. It is all about the details. The most important details are found in the choice of entry and exit routes. I am going to beat on this subject until you are sick of it.

That is what separated Dan, Larry and me — the amount of time we spent thinking about and planning our stand locations to take maximum advantage of a low-profile entry and exit. As another of my friends so accurately put things, "If someone was going to try to sneak into your house, they wouldn't come up the front door beating a bass drum."

BUILD YOUR HUNT BACKWARDS

Think about your hunting in a different, possibly even radical, way. Rather than focusing on the spots with the best sign, ignore the deer sign during your next scouting trip. That's right; totally ignore it. Instead, spend all your time figuring out how you can get into your hunting area and then out of it again without alerting a single deer. Try it. I think you will be amazed by how much differently you start to think about deer hunting. This really should be your number one priority.

Look for any route where you can stay out of sight, the perfect path so that your scent doesn't blow to the deer; anywhere you can walk where you don't make noise. Put it all together and that is the route you need to take. Finding the perfect path should be your number one goal on your next scouting trip. It likely won't be the easiest route, and that is why many will never use this approach. Doing things right isn't for the lazy.

Now that I have hopefully piqued your interest in finding the low-profile hunter highways into and out of your area, I will next take a closer look at how creeks and ditches, specifically, fit into this strategy.

The Best Entry and Exit Routes

Rod Ponton, a friend of the author, shot this great buck from a stand he accessed by using the edge of a hog lot and then dropping down into a deep creek. When someone puts this much thought into the route he takes to get to his stands, you can bet he understands the fine points of deer hunting.

As I stressed in the last chapter, choosing the best route to and from each stand is the most important detail in structuring a good season. Casual hunters rarely consider this critical aspect of the hunt. When they talk about their stands, they talk about deer sign. Whenever seasoned hunters talk about a stand location, they are much more likely to talk first about how they get to and from it — the entry and exit routes.

I remember a stand I hunted clear back in the early 90s that belonged to a friend of mine in Kansas. Rod spent 20 minutes explaining exactly how he accessed the stand. While that may not seem like a big deal, he did that while we were sitting in his truck on a county road with the stand just 200 yards away in plain sight! The route included parking in the neighbor's driveway, sneaking past his pig pen, crawling through some shatter cane and then into a creek where you had to go hand to hand along the high bank of the creek holding on to roots to keep from slipping into the deep pool.

Finally, at the base of the tree, it was a simple matter to climb up out of the creek and right into the stand. By the time Rod was done explaining how to get in there undetected, I knew I was hunting with the right person. Anyone who understands the importance of a clean entry route is a person who understands the importance of details.

WINNING THE CHESS MATCH

Think about it this way: you spook a doe on the way to your stand. She runs off 100 yards and stands and snorts for five minutes. Every deer within 300-400 yards knows something is wrong. The number of deer you'll see that day definitely goes down, and the older, wiser ones are the first to heed the doe's warning.

Now suppose that she doesn't blow, but comes stalking back two hours later looking for you. Maybe for the next several days she is tense in that area. Her body language alone is enough to make other deer nervous around your stand. They know when a doe is nervous she is nervous for a reason, and they pay attention. It is like she is saying, "Beware, there is danger here." Spooking even non-target deer is a disease that quickly spreads and consumes otherwise great stands.

Again, as I said, I am going to beat this until you are sick of it, but my hope is that it really sinks in. It might be easier to understand if I put this in human terms. Let's say you are sitting in your car in a parking lot getting ready to go into the 7-Eleven for a Snickers Ice Cream Bar (I love those things). Just as you are opening the

You may think you can get away with crossing open fields in the pre-dawn semi-darkness without alarming deer. However, you may not even realize the damage you have done because not all deer snort and stomp off. They may merely sneak away, yet your location has been compromised in a very real way.

We have all sat in dead stands over the years. Sometimes we are just in the wrong place, but other times it is the result of alerting a mature doe or two upon entry. Through their body language, these deer tell all others in the area that danger is near.

door to get out, someone comes running out of the store screaming, "Danger! Danger! Look out!" You wouldn't rush right into the store. You would stay back and watch for a long time until you knew things were fine, or you would simply drive somewhere else to get your ice cream.

Do you think deer are so dumb that they don't recognize warning signals from other deer? They are more tuned in to survival than we are. They recognize warning signals we may not even realize exist.

I've sat in several dead stands through the years, wondering why I wasn't seeing deer. The answer often showed up an hour after sunrise when a lone doe came sneaking toward me in super-slow motion to check things out. She'd obviously been somewhere nearby when I approached and wasn't going to leave the area until she knew what I was up to. It is amazing how patient a mature doe can be when she's trying to sort out danger. Unfortunately, every deer that comes into the area will see her tense and focused body language and slink off without ever coming past.

Do everything you can to get in clean. Take advantage of terrain and cover to keep out of sight as much as possible. Even in the dark, deer can see a skylined hunter, so keep to low ground. Ravines, deep ditches and creeks are ideal.

Your mental map of your hunting area should be marked and sliced up with lines indicating the low-profile access routes you will use to get in and out clean. In other words, you need to take full advantage of all the creeks and ditches.

WHY CREEKS AND DITCHES ARE BEST

Bar none, creeks and ditches are my favorite terrain features to use when access-

Creeks and ditches should be such an important part of your hunting strategy that you will go out of your way to find them and build your entire game plan around the access routes they offer and the deer travel patterns they produce.

ing my stands. Remember, I talked about working backwards to find great stand sites. I love them so much that I will go out of my way to find stands near creeks and ditches just so I can use the low ground to slip into and out of my hunting area.

Since you are below the general lay of the land, the deer are less likely to see you as you pass. Also, the sounds you make are muffled by the close walls of the terrain. Since the wind blows over these features, your scent is not as likely to wash around the area. Finally, you are walking in an area that deer are not likely to frequent (they may cross them, but they typically don't walk right down a ditch) so your ground scent won't be discovered easily.

Obviously, this is the definition of a perfect entry and exit route. To make these locations even better, I will go in ahead of the season with a chainsaw and remove any brush or blown down timber that has fallen into the creek or ditch so my passage can be quieter, quicker and more enjoyable.

In Chapter 5, I will go into detail about how to read a topographic map, but let me quickly offer a preview on creeks and ditches. Creeks that flow most of the year are unbroken blue lines on the map while seasonal creeks are broken blue lines.

Ditches are often harder to see because you have to interpret the contour lines to anticipate where they may lie, but with some practice, you can see them easily. Stacked V-shaped contour lines are generally ravines. When the lines are stacked comparatively close together, the ravine is steep, and steep ravines generally have ditches on their bottoms, especially in farm country where soil erosion is common. Looking for these features makes it easy to find creeks and ditches without ever walking a property. As I get into reading these maps, this discussion will all make more sense.

DON'T OVERLOOK EXIT ROUTES

I've been focusing almost entirely on entry routes, but if you intend to hunt that part of the property more than once, your exit route is just as important. If you spook deer as you leave your stand, it will reduce your odds next time you hunt it. In many cases, your exit route will be different from your entry route. Keep in mind where the deer will likely be at the time you walk out and go well out of your way to avoid these areas. Again, focusing on terrain features such as creeks and ditches will help you keep a low profile.

When hunting the edges of feeding areas, you will find it very tough to get out cleanly at the end of legal shooting time. This is one of the most difficult challenges in deer hunting. I have had very good success in the past few years arranging for someone to drive in and bump the deer off the field with a vehicle (or better yet, a tractor) at the end of legal shooting time. If the deer are used to some human activity in the area, they will forgive this maneuver quickly. I would not do it every day for a week, but a few times per week will not affect the feeding habits of the deer. They keep right on schedule.

If you have to sneak out in the absence of creeks or ditches, look for anything in the terrain or cover that will keep you hidden from nearby deer. It is hard to find any other features as good as creeks and ditches, and that is why I go out of my

Creeks and ditches offer the perfect entry and exit routes because the deer can't easily see, hear or smell you when you slip along the bottoms of these terrain features.

way to hunt near them. Sometimes a ravine is present, and even without a ditch at the bottom, it at least serves to keep me off the skyline. I have also used steep bluffs as my exit routes. I can drop off the side of the bluff and disappear in just a step or two.

Sometimes you will find thick cover that you can sneak along, like a brushy fence line or even a field of standing corn, but outside of these few examples, it can be tough to find truly low-profile exit routes (and entry routes, for that matter). You may need to make your own. That is what I am going to get into in the next chapter.

Creating Your Own Low-Profile Entry and Exit Routes

Standing crops such as corn or forage sorghum grow tall enough that you can sneak behind them to reach your stands. If you have the ability to plant screen plots such as these, or the farmer is late in removing tall crops, you have a great way to get in and out cleanly.

I realize I am getting a bit off topic here, but I think the tangent is worth a short chapter. This book is really about becoming a better deer hunter, and while we are on the subject of using creeks and ditches for entry and exit, it is worth a side trip into the subject of creative alternatives you can use in their absence.

Not every part of your hunting area will have good entry and exit routes. That means you have two options; either avoid hunting those areas or create your own routes. I have had good luck creating them and some of my friends have turned this into a fine art. Here are a few of the strategies that have worked.

Standing crops: This is the easiest method and one of the most effective. If you have to cover open ground, it makes sense to get double duty out of your screen by planting a tall food source. I plant corn in these areas now, but I have also used forage sorghum (as opposed to grain sorghum) in areas with high deer numbers. The deer won't eat the sorghum when it is growing, so it gains its full height and puts on a decent grain head before the deer start to pull it down and feed on it. Corn, on the other hand, is like candy to deer during the summer. So, if you have a large deer population you may find that they have eaten your screen to the ground by late July!

Tree plantings: I have a friend who used a tree mover to place cedar trees into a double row that permits him to slip through open areas undetected. I have looked it over, and it really is slick. Larry is a master of this kind of stuff.

Granted, you need access to dozens (maybe even hundreds) of trees if you are going to build a sizeable cedar screen, but I can't imagine a better way to slip around the edge of a feeding area than through a tunnel of cedar trees. The trees are dense, block the wind and their needles rarely fall off. Even a few trees planted in the right spots can make a big difference as you sneak away from a food source, for example.

If you can't move them in, you can still plant them. It will take about 10 years for a two-foot cedar seedling to reach six or seven feet tall, but if you don't start now, you will always wish you had. As the old saying goes, "The best time to plant a tree is 10 years ago. The second-best time is today."

You have two options when it comes to planting trees to form screens. One option is to plant good-sized seedlings that will produce cover fairly quickly, as shown here. Be sure to cage the small trees to keep the bucks from killing them by rubbing or browsing.

A second option when creating permanent screens is to plant the trees from seeds. Normally, this refers to tilling the ground to create a good seedbed and then planting acorns or other conveniently available tree seeds, including cedar.

Switchgrass: Switchgrass makes a good screen if you take care of it properly. It likes good soils and fertilizer, so just throwing a few seeds out is not going to get it done. I have planted Cave-In-Rock switchgrass on some of the land I have managed over the years and have some on the farm we currently own. If left to nature, it will not grow much over about four to five feet tall. To get it to reach its maximum "screen" height of about six feet, you need to take good care of it. Consult with an agronomist about proper switchgrass maintenance in your area. That will include fertilizer, other soil prep such as liming and timely burning to clean up competition.

Building berms: I am not a big fan of using a bulldozer to create screens, but I have seen it done. Typically, this is a long mound along the edge of a field or food plot behind which the hunter sneaks. It doesn't have to be more than two to three feet tall, because brush will grow on top and make the screen naturally taller. Plus, you can walk in the borrow ditch that is naturally made as you push up the berm. Basically, you just push the dirt from the outside of the field inward, creating a narrow, shallow ditch in which you walk while the dirt forms the berm behind which you hide.

If you have access to a bulldozer (or even a skid loader) and can't come up with a good way to get past deer as you head to and from your stands, this method will definitely work and doesn't create too much of an eyesore. Just be sure to provide some form of drainage to keep the shallow ditch from pooling water after a rain.

Specialized seed blends: I have had the opportunity to experiment with a blend called Plot Screen from Frigid Forage. This stuff grows eight to 10 feet tall and very thick so that only a 10-foot wide band will be enough to keep you hidden from nearby deer. It is an annual, so you will have to plant it every year. Other planted screens may also work, but this stuff is ready to go and you can plant it well into June in many areas and still get a good stand.

OFFBEAT ENTRY AND EXIT TRICKS

It takes creative thinking to come up with the best access routes for your stands. That's one of the most enjoyable aspects of preparing for the coming season: the chess match of getting in and out. You can

It only takes two years to establish a good stand of switchgrass. Where soils are good, it can grow as much as 6 feet tall, creating a very effective screen that will last for many years.

take things even farther if you think way outside the box. Here are a couple of tricks that should get you thinking creatively.

Wait until first light to access certain morning stands: Last year was a very dry fall, and I confirmed to myself that waiting until I could see the ground was the best morning entry strategy. It eliminated the need for a flashlight, and I was able to move much faster. Deer are more sensitive to the sneaking crunch, pause, crunch than they are to a more rapid cadence. The ability to see the ground also permits you to miss those branches that will snap loudly. Break up your footfalls to sound more like a four-legged animal. Raking a path through the leaves is also a great option.

A surprising number of hunters believe deer can't see them in the dark as they cross an open field to get to their morning stands. And others feel deer don't react to human encounters during the dark. Well, I've got some bad news. Not only can they see us, hear us and smell us under most nighttime conditions, but they don't quickly forgive these intrusions. When you are forced to cross an open field (as opposed to coming in from the backside) where deer might be feeding in the morning, wait until first light so you can avoid any deer that are still out in the open.

Arrange a diversion: I have already mentioned this one, but it is worth mentioning again. When you're hunting along the edge of a feeding area, it can be nearly impossible to get back to your vehicle in the evening without spooking deer. If they see you climb out of a treestand or ground blind, or hear you crunching around in the timber nearby, they'll be very reluctant to use the area again.

If you're hunting an open field, either keep your stand well back from the edge where you can slip out and down a ditch — or similar feature — or arrange for someone to drive up to the stand at the end of legal shooting time and move the deer off naturally.

Run to your stand: With crunching, ankle-deep leaves everywhere, my friend knew he couldn't sneak in to his afternoon stand located just below a bedding ridge. So, he decided to make the crunching leaves work for him instead of against him.

The solution was true genius. My friend took a solid grip on his bow and crashed through the woods at a dead run — right to the base of the tree. He tried to sound as much like a buck chasing a doe as he possibly could, cracking limbs and generally making a racket. After climbing quickly to his stand, my friend was settled for less

If you wait until the faintest first light to approach your morning stands, you can often avoid deer feeding in open areas and move quickly with less noise.

It can be difficult to get away from some stands near feeding areas when deer are nearby. Rather than risk alerting them and making them leery of your stand sites, arrange to have someone drive up in a vehicle or ATV to move them out of the area before you climb down or exit your ground blind.

than a minute when a giant, long-tined, 8-pointer came off the ridge to investigate. The shot was only 10 yards as the buck freshened a scrape right under the tree!

CONCLUSION

As you can see, coming up with access options can be fun but often labor intensive and even expensive. It is so much better to take maximum advantage of what nature supplies: the creeks and ditches that already carve up your hunting area.

I can't overstate my key point here: the most important consideration when selecting a stand site is undetected access. Some properties have ample creeks and ditches that you can and should discover. Without a doubt, learning to use them on every level possible will make you a much better deer hunter.

It's All About Funnels

The author's long-time friend, Mike Sawyer, took this great main-frame 8-pointer during the 2008 season from a stand located in a long, narrow finger of trees that deer use to access the open fields nearby. Such funnels make for great bow stands.

This book isn't about hunting funnels, at least not in the strictest sense, but anytime you set out to hunt whitetails, funnels are always part of the chess match. The goal of this book is to help you shoot more mature bucks and providing an education in Funnels 101 will set the groundwork for when I get into a more detailed discourse on terrain and particularly how creeks and ditches influence deer movement.

Hunting the terrain is all about recognizing and hunting funnels. So, it would be impossible to write this book and make it useful without spending some time digging into the subject of funnels — in their broadest sense and then as they relate to the terrain and finally as they relate to creeks and ditches.

Hunting funnels is one of the most basic of all deer-hunting strategies. It is also one of the most effective. I hunt a wide range of stand types now, but when I first started bowhunting, I bet 75 percent of my stands were on funnels and those were always my best ones. You can be a very successful bowhunter without a ton of knowledge about local deer patterns if you have a nose for finding all the funnels.

Funnels allow you to simplify your deer hunting to the point where you really don't need to know the patterns of any specific deer. Think about that. You don't really need to know what bucks are around or where they feed or even where they bed. You only need to know that at certain times they will be on the move and when they do move, they will be using funnels often.

You only need to find narrow places that will appeal to one of their two priorities when traveling: the desire to keep a low profile and the desire to take the path of least resistance. I will come back and focus on terrain features that meet these priorities, but first I want to cover the fundamentals — making sure you understand exactly what a funnel is and how diverse they can be.

THE BASICS

Funnels are simple to understand. Some people call them bottlenecks, and that is an appropriate name too. If there are deer trails, the funnel is the neck of the

Funnels are simple to find once you start thinking about it. Anything that bottlenecks traveling deer will increase your chance for success. Look for funnels created by both the terrain and cover.

Hunting funnels makes it easier to keep deer from getting downwind of you while on stand. The same features of the terrain or cover that bottleneck the deer also give you a safe direction for your scent to blow.

hourglass where the trails converge before spreading back out. By hunting funnels, you accomplish two things. First, you bring more deer within range of your bow or gun. That is a simple matter of playing the odds. You don't have to be an MIT graduate to understand that the more deer that come within range, the better your chances for filling a tag.

Second, and less obviously, hunting funnels makes it easier to keep deer from getting downwind of you, smelling you and spoiling your hunt. Because the funnel pulls those trails in, there are simply less trails on the downwind side (assuming you hunt with the wind at a 90-degree angle to the funnel). Funnels make it easier to put together a surgical strategy because you know where the deer won't be. That is just as important as knowing where they will be.

Does use funnels more than bucks, but bucks will use them too. Bucks are more likely to go from Point A to Point B by the most direct route — the shortest path — than does. Bucks also seem to be naturally wary of funnels in the same sense that animals are wary of waterholes. They may sense that they are vulnerable in these places. I have shot plenty of bucks in funnels, but just understand that not every buck will just waltz right through these spots.

Despite any downside, funnels remain a key stand location for taking bucks during all parts of the season. Now let's take a look at the types of funnels you are likely to find.

COVER-RELATED FUNNELS

It is pretty easy to see cover-related funnels by studying an aerial photo of your hunting area. In fact, we are going to dig into aerial photos a bit more before this book is finished, so a quick understanding of what they can teach is in order. Aerial photos are simply that — photos taken from the air. Normally they are taken at a very slight angle or straight down so the lay of the land is not easily discerned. If the photos are taken in the morning or evening you can see shadows in the valleys giving some insight into the terrain itself, but if the photo is taken with the sun straight overhead, those features become very hard to see.

Keeping this simple, aerial photos show us the

When looking at areas with lots of patchy cover, you will likely find your best stand sites in the small, narrow corridors that connect them, such as fence lines and even standing crop fields.

cover. If you want to study the terrain specifically, you will need topographic maps. More about topo maps later, when I get deeper into terrain-related funnels.

WHERE TO GET AERIAL PHOTOS:

The Internet offers the very best source for aerial photos and topographic maps. I have a number of favorite websites I use for viewing my hunting area, but the simplest one I have found is MapCard.com. If I want to purchase a large, laminated map or photo, I go to MyTopo. com. You can do an online search and find literally dozens of great sources for both maps and photos. Most of them work off the same database; usually the photos are very recent.

How to read an aerial photo: It is harder to determine the terrain when looking at an aerial photo than when looking at a topo map. However, aerial photos have tremendous value. They show the cover more specifically than do topo maps. Aerial photos also show large-scale terrain features, such as ravines, ridges and creeks reasonably well. You can see these features by looking at the shading in the photo; it gives away terrain features and permits a sort of three-dimensional view.

Aerial photos are best at showing the cover, but they can also display some features of the terrain if they are large enough to cause shading in the image. In this wide-view aerial photo, you can see many areas where the cover narrows down, encouraging any deer traveling in that area to come past within easy range.

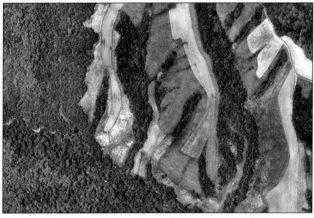

In this blown up section from the larger aerial photo, you can see the stand site the author used for nine seasons while hunting this property. It is a classic, cover-related bottleneck.

Aerial photos also show manmade details such as trails, buildings, fence lines and brush piles much more clearly than topo maps. These are all very important parts of an effective hunting strategy. To have a complete view of your hunting area, you need both a topo map and an aerial photo.

Though they don't reveal the terrain in detail, aerial photos are a tremendous tool for scouting and hunting. I still use them every year on the farms I hunt. As I have already said, a good stand location allows you to play the wind not only while you're sitting in it, but also while you're entering and exiting. Aerial photos allow you to plan entry and exit routes very carefully.

Cover-related funnels are very easy to understand and to find. They are much easier to figure out than terrain-related funnels. If you look at the aerial photo, you will see them immediately. Any thin strip of cover connecting two larger blocks is a good candidate for a tree-stand. See how easy that is?

They jump right off the photo.

But not all cover-related funnels are created equal. Some are better than others because the deer have a more obvious reason to use them. The same is true of any type of funnel. A classic example is a brushy fence line between two woodlots that always hold family groups. During the rut, bucks will cruise back and forth between the woodlots. Another example is a simple bottleneck where two blocks of cover meet at their corners.

During the early and late seasons, the best funnels are those that lie between bedding areas and feeding areas. Think of a slough leading from a creek bottom up to a picked cornfield. The deer will take that path.

Cover-related funnels are simple — too simple to write an entire book about, so they won't be part of this series. I mention them here just to give some context to the real purpose of this book, and that is to find and exploit terrain-related funnels.

TERRAIN-RELATED FUNNELS

Once we get into the subject of evaluating the terrain to determine where deer are likely to move, we open a very broad subject. Not only is this subject big enough for a book, we are taking the position that it is big enough for a series of books. There are many different terrain features, and each of them has a slightly different influence on deer movement. While deer may not always use a certain feature the same way every time they encounter it, there are tendencies we can exploit.

All we can do when pre-dicting how deer will move is to focus on these tendencies. As I have already said, we must play the odds. Over time, this strategy will pay off and you will be more consistently successful. There is no such thing as a behavior deer always exhibit — except maybe to run from us! However, I even question that one. I have seen deer that didn't run from me. One time, a curious 6-pointer followed me all the way to the tree I was going to hunt, staying just 30 yards behind me. He stood there and watched as I put the stand up and then finally when I was all done, he stomped around, snorted and bolted off as if I had shocked him with a prod!

So, the point is there is nothing deer do 100 percent of the time. The way they use the terrain is no different. There will be times an old buck will jump right off a high bank into a creek to cross it rather than take the convenient crossing nearby. When they do what they aren't supposed to do, you will shake your head, curse me for writing this book and think about giving up on this terrain-hunting thing.

Bill Winke shot this great buck from the stand shown in the blow-up of the aerial photo on the previous page. It was his biggest buck at the time. From that day on, he was sold on hunting funnels during the rut.

Don't do it. By focusing on the tendencies, you are playing the odds and that is all you can ever do. There is no perfect strategy.

WHY DEER USE TERRAIN PREDICTABLY

As I have already mentioned, the word "predictable" is relative. Deer use terrain somewhat predictably for a couple reasons. When traveling, deer look for ways to make the trip easier and safer. It doesn't really matter why they use these terrain features; it only matters that they do. One or the other of these two reasons will generally apply. You don't really need to know what is going on inside the deer's head. You only have to know you are hunting a place they like to travel through.

SUBTLE FUNNELS

Not all funnels are easy to spot; some of them are very subtle. These are generally related to slight breaks in the terrain, but at times these subtle funnels can be something as simple as an open gate that entices traveling deer or a fallen tree that nudges them to the edge of a ridge. Keep your eyes open when scouting and

Funnels caused by the terrain are very common in areas with hills and valleys. Many parts of the whitetail's range have these rough-ground features. Deer use them in a more or less predictable way.

you will start to see not only the obvious terrain and cover-related funnels, but the subtle ones too. Once you settle on the overall area where you want to place your stand, the subtle features will help you fine-tune the location until you are in the perfect killing tree.

Negative terrain features, such as the edge of a bluff, show us where a deer won't go. That means that on the edge of this feature there should be a well-worn trail representing the funnel formed by all the deer diverting their travels to bypass the feature. This is why terrain features are so good at funneling deer, because the deer are very predictable in their desire to find the path of least resistance.

How to Read a Topographic Map

Bill Winke's friend, Mike Sawyer, shot this heavy-antlered buck from a ridge-top stand where deer traditionally come to bed. The buck was looking for does late in the rut when he came past the stand. Being able to identify such spots from simply studying topographic maps will make you a better deer hunter.

You can find funnels all over the place, and you don't even have to walk the area to see them. If you don't have time to scout on foot or don't want to contaminate your hunting area with a bunch of in-season scouting, you can easily find funnels by studying topographic maps and aerial photos.

I have already mentioned some simple tips for reading aerial photos, but figuring out what all the lines on a topo map mean is a bit hairier. In this chapter, I am going to focus on helping you learn to pull all the information you can from topo maps.

Take a close look at the map below. You will see lots of curving parallel lines, white spaces, green spaces and blue lines. Those are the elements of a topo map, and by understanding their roles you can determine good places to hang stands. It sounds strange, doesn't it? A few lines on paper can tell you where the deer travel? It is true. And since we know deer relate to terrain in predictable ways, we just need to find familiar terrain features to predict deer movement in any area. It really does work. I have done this many times and shot big deer as a result of nothing more than just reading a map. Let's get started.

WHITE AND GREEN SPACES

The white areas on topographic maps are open fields. The green areas are timber or thick (permanent) cover. In my experience, these colored areas of a topo map are not very accurate. In other words, I wouldn't determine that a saddle was in the timber just because it appears to be in a green area on a topo map. The white and green areas appear to be woefully outdated on most topo maps. I don't believe the makers of these maps cross-check them with current habitat and cover conditions on a regular basis, meaning that a map created in 1950 might still be showing the cover that was present then, even though the setting is completely different now.

Therefore, do not trust the white and green spaces on your topo maps. The true value of topo maps is their ability to depict the terrain. If you are serious

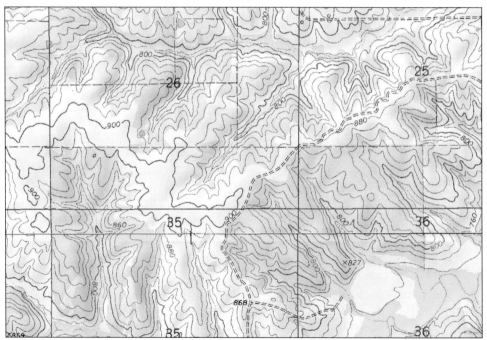

Topographic maps can appear intimidating when you first look at them, with lines snaking all over the place. However, if you will take the time to study the map you will soon start to see terrain features jump off the page and eventually start to see deer movement patterns take shape. All it takes is practice.

about the cover, you will need to study a very current aerial photo.

BLUE LINES

The blue lines are streams or run-off areas. If the blue line is solid, the waterway is more or less permanent, such as a creek or river. Obviously, drought years can make an impact on stream flow, but if you think of the solid blue lines as streams that carry water, most of the time you will be accurate.

If the blue lines are dashed, they depict streams

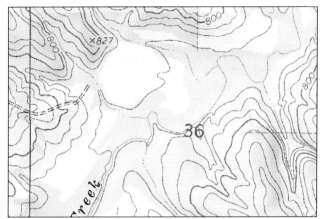

In this image you can see many of the common symbols on a topographic map: creeks (in this case the solid blue line indicates a creek that carries water year-round and the dashed blue lines indicate seasonal creeks), green spaces (theoretically these are cover) and white spaces, which are supposed to represent open areas.

or waterways that are seasonal, such as creeks that only flow during the spring or ditches that only carry water shortly after a rain.

I study these lines all the time. They have much to tell. First, I want to know where the water is. Deer need reliable water sources in dry years. So, if nothing else, the solid blue lines suggest where they might find it. This is important information because pools in these streams and creeks (even if the flow has stopped) will represent important water sources keeping deer in a certain area, or even suggesting a good place to hang your stand in dry conditions.

Second, I want to know if a certain waterway is a likely entry or exit route I can use to keep a low profile going to and from my stands. Seasonal waterways (those represented by broken lines) tend to be easier to walk through because in a typical fall they are dry. You don't have to splash through water as you slip along the bottom of a ditch, for example. Don't ignore

When a creek makes a sharp bend, that normally signals a high bank on the outside of the bend. Deer don't like to cross at this high bank. When two of these bends fall close together – forming an S shape – the deer are likely to cross on the gradual bank in the middle between the two bends. A straight stretch of waterway normally doesn't contain many funnels as the deer can, and do, cross almost anywhere.

solid blue lines as potential entry and exit routes, but the dashed lines will generally end up being more appealing.

Third, the twisting and turning of the waterway, whether seasonal or permanent, will suggest places where the deer will cross it. Where the waterway makes an S-curve, the deer will tend to cross at the middle of the S. The bends tend to indicate high banks in most areas. They are caused by erosion as the waterway curves and cuts away the loose soil, leaving a high bank or sharp drop-off.

Anytime you have a straight stretch of waterway between two bends, you have a likely crossing — a funnel between two high banks. The terrain change itself may not be great enough to show up in the contour lines of the topo map. Either way, you can be sure that high banks occur on most bends in the waterway and deer will avoid crossing where the bank is high, preferring the easier passage nearby. This easier passage creates what might be the perfect place for your treestand during the rut, as bucks cruise from one doe bedding area to another.

CONTOUR LINES

We have covered a lot so far in this chapter, but the most important aspects of topo maps remain — the curving contour lines you see looping all over the map. Their secrets are critical to understanding deer movement.

Contour lines are simple on the surface. They signify all the places on land you are studying that lie at the same elevation. If you look at the lines, you will

Southern Minnesota bowhunter Bill Clink has taken a number of really nice bucks by focusing on terrain in the rugged bluff country he hunts. You can often find great stands after doing little more than studying a topo map.

see that some have numbers on them — that is the elevation reading for that line. Normally, contour lines signify a difference of 20 feet of elevation change. So, every line indicates an elevation that is 20 feet above or 20 feet below the nearest line. The scale can change on some maps, so study the numbers to determine the scale of the map you are looking at.

Getting back to what contour lines mean, if you could take an altimeter and walk around the land in a way that prevents any changes in the elevation reading on your instrument, you would be perfectly following a contour line.

Knowing the elevation of a spot doesn't really tell you much, so you have to look to the shape of the lines and proximity of adjacent lines (how close they are to each other) to reveal the subtle aspects of the terrain that allow us to visualize terrain features and predict deer movement.

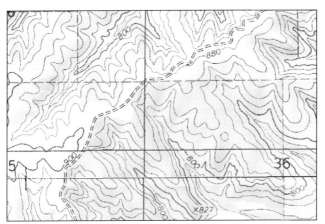

The lane shown near the top of this topographic map is on the ridge top. The contour lines you see pointing up toward it from the bottom are ravines cutting into the ridge. Ridges and ravines are classic terrain features in most whitetail country.

Shape of Contour Lines: It takes a little imagination and mental visualization skills to understand what the shape of a contour line means about the terrain it describes. I will paint this picture for you, but you will have to be patient and really apply yourself as this takes some study to understand clearly. Ultimately, you should be able to see features jumping off the map as if they were in 3-D. In fact, if you get a chance, do an online search for "shaded relief topo maps" and look at a few of them. The subtle shading of these maps makes it easier to see the actual lay of the land — they appear three-dimensional, making it much easier to visualize the terrain.

One way you can think about a contour line is to consider it as a slice. If you took a slice at a certain elevation and just removed all the land above that slice, the outside edge of this flat plateau would be the contour line at that elevation.

Here are a few specific features: When the contour lines make a jut toward the inside (toward the middle if you are looking at just that one line) you are looking at a ditch or ravine. Think about it; if you are walking along a side hill and then reach a draw coming down off the ridge, you will have to turn in toward the ridge to stay at the same elevation. If you keep going straight, you will drop off into the ravine. So, a dimple inward is a valley, ditch or ravine.

Conversely, a dimple outward is a ridge or point leading away from the main ridge. Again, if you are walking along a side hill and come to a secondary ridge leading to the side, you will have to walk away from the main ridge to stay on the same elevation. If you keep going straight, you will walk up and over the secondary ridge.

A rough circle or oval on the topo map is either a dip or a knob; it's a dip if it descends and a knob if it ascends. You can tell easily which one it is by studying adjacent contour lines. If the numbers ascend as you get away from the circle, you are looking at a dip. The opposite holds true, of course, if the numbers descend on either side of the circular contour line.

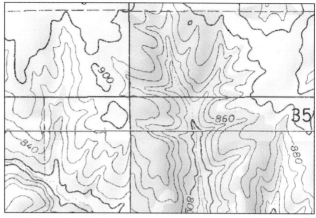

In this section of topo map you can see two saddles (high points) in the ridge (on the left side of the image). The top of the ridge is at 900 feet and there are two circular contour lines of the same elevation isolated on the ridge, representing high spots. There are two saddles here; one in the gap above the 900 symbol and one in the gap below it. Deer use saddles when crossing ridges to keep a low profile and reduce the effort required to cross.

Proximity of Contour Lines: You can tell a lot about the steepness of the terrain by looking at how close the contour lines are to each other. Since adjacent lines typically describe points that are 20 feet apart in elevation, the closer the lines are to each other, the steeper the terrain is in that area. Where they are far apart, the land is flat or has a very gentle slope.

You can use this method to see ridge tops, flat fields, bluff edges and even steep banks along rivers or creeks.

By studying a topo map, keeping these rules in mind, you will soon start to see terrain features that jump right out at you. Eventually, you will pick out each feature of the property with ease. Try it and you will see. Next, when you apply some knowledge of how deer relate to common features, you can even anticipate how they will move through the property without ever setting foot on it.

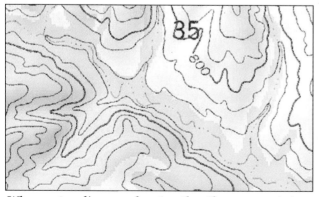

When contour lines are close together, they represent steep drop-offs. When they are spread well apart, they represent areas that are flat or nearly flat. In the bottom part of this image, you can see a bluff edge where the lines are close together just on the south side of the creek.

In the next chapter, I am going to show you how you can identify some common terrain features using topo maps and what these features mean. Even though the focus of this book is creeks and ditches, the goal of this section is learning to read and apply the knowledge found on topo maps. I am going to diverge a bit. My plan is to show you how the topo map really makes you a better deer hunter.

Chapter 6

Classic Terrain Funnels

Terrain affects how deer move through any piece of property. This goes well beyond just creeks and ditches. In this chapter the author discusses several other common terrain features and how they influence deer patterns.

In this chapter, I am going to touch briefly on a wide range of terrain features that aren't affected by creeks and ditches. I will save my full discussion on creeks and ditches for coming chapters. Here are a few common terrain features, how you find them and how deer use them.

WOODED SADDLE

You can identify a saddle easily on a topo map, but it is nearly impossible to see on an aerial photo. On the topo map, look for a gap between two opposite bends in contour lines at the same elevation. For example, saddles often look like two ovals (or the ends of two ovals) next to each other. Their narrow ends will point toward one another. The contour lines on most topo maps are 20 feet apart, so you can get some indication of the depth of a saddle from the number of ovals stacked up on top of each other on either side of the gap.

Even subtle saddles can be good deer funnels, because cruising bucks are quick to look for anything to keep their profile low and keep them off the skyline. I have seen heavy trails through saddles barely five feet deep. These, unfortunately, you will often have to find through traditional scouting because their depth is too shallow to show up on a topo map.

The next step in finding a great saddle stand is to determine whether the location is within the timber or out in the open. While deer will use this feature in both situations, you will find better action during the middle of the day if the saddle is in the timber. You need only look at the aerial photo to determine the type of cover surrounding the saddle.

When hunting a saddle initially, set your stand in a safe spot where deer are not likely to smell you. You can always get more aggressive with stand placement as you learn how the deer use the saddle. Consider hugging one side of the saddle or the other, well up the slope so that the wind is steadier and more predictable, carrying your scent in a consistent direction. Swirling winds will always be your

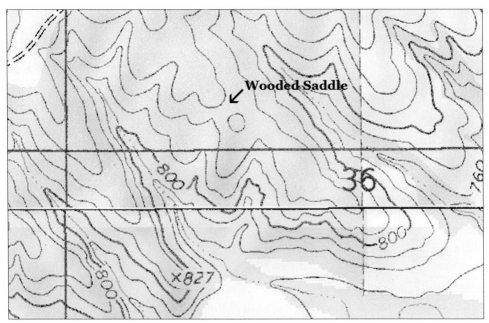

A wooded saddle is a classic funnel. It is seen as a low area on a ridgeline. You can see it on a topo map as a gap between adjacent contour lines. Normally, the saddle will appear as a gap between ovals or round circles on the topo map, as seen here.

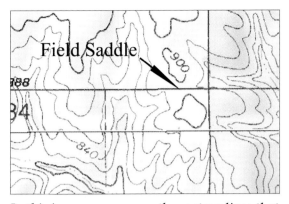

In this image, you can see the contour lines that represent a field-crossing saddle. This is a very well-used deer funnel. Without looking at an aerial photo of the area, you have to assume the saddle is in the open field. However, topo maps are not the best source of cover information so it is wise to cross-check the area using a recent aerial photo.

This is the aerial photo that goes with the topographic map of the field-crossing saddle. It is easy to confirm here that the ridge top is in fact an open field. You can also clearly see how tough it is to see the terrain variations when looking at an aerial photo. From the photo alone, it would be very hard to guess there is a saddle in this location. Thorough map scouting requires both a topographic map and an aerial photo.

enemy when hunting broken terrain, so set up initially with an eye toward eliminating swirling. Normally, that means you have to be close to the top of the ridge. So, dropping off just over the side into the saddle is a reasonably conservative first stand choice.

As you learn more about what the deer are doing — and how the wind swirls for any given direction — you can adjust your stand site.

FIELD-CROSSING SADDLE

The field-crossing saddle is another classic travel route. Many people call such spots swales. It is a saddle in an open, ridge-top field. Wooded ravines on both sides of the ridge usually extend toward each other, creating the ideal place for a buck to cross the ridgeline. A buck wanting to travel from one side of the ridge to the other is likely to use this crossing point to keep a low profile. It is a common rut travel pattern among bucks.

Again, you can find this saddle easily with the topo map and then confirm that it is, in fact, a field saddle instead of a wooded saddle by looking at the aerial photo. The wooded draw pointing toward each other from either side of a typical field crossing saddle would be equally good as a stand choice. However, it would be best to make that decision after you look at this saddle first hand. You can base your choice on the field of view and the availability of trees with enough cover to hide your form. A steady wind is also important, so the side that is higher, and therefore offers a more consistent wind flow, would be the better choice.

BLUFF EDGE

You can see a bluff easily on a topo map, but it is harder to see on an aerial photo. The contour lines of the topo map will be very close together, signifying a steep slope. The steeper the slope, the more effective the bluff is at funneling deer movement. So, I am always on the lookout for places on the topo map where the lines are very close together.

Deer follow edges. They also try to reduce the amount of work involved in getting from Point A to Point B. Any deer (bucks included) moving along a sidehill will funnel right along the bluff edge if the slope is steep enough. Very rarely will they travel a near-vertical slope.

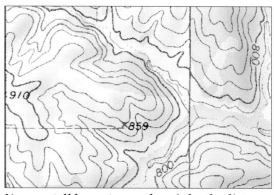

You can tell how steep a slope is by the distance between contour lines on a topo map. The closer they are, the steeper the slope. Deer avoid super-steep slopes and will detour to the top of the slope to go around them. This produces a good funnel.

This image shows a long, fairly flat ridge that is covered with trees. In most parts of the whitetail's range, this would be the classic bedding ridge. Whitetails like to bed high so they can see danger easily. The spot at the head of the draw that cuts into the ridge from the northwest is an ideal spot for a treestand.

Bluff stands are among my favorites because they offer some incredible advantages. You can place your stand near the edge of the bluff and then hunt it with the wind blowing out over the bluff. There is no way a deer will be able to smell you when you set up this way. If you can climb the bluff from below to reach your stand, you have the ultimate setup; one where the deer never detect your entry or exit and never smell you on stand. Some of the bluffs I have hunted in the past were so steep I couldn't climb straight to the stand location. So, I climbed a more gradual part of the slope and hugged the bluff edge to my stand.

In most areas with broken ground (especially in areas with some agriculture), there will be fields on the ridges and fields in the bottoms and the hillsides will be covered with trees. With that in mind, you can often find funnels along the edges of ridge-top fields where these fields come close to a bluff edge. That makes for a very nice, tight funnel that deer use throughout the year, but one that bucks especially use during the rut.

Bluff stands are among the author's favorites because they funnel deer while also providing a safe place for human scent to blow where no deer are likely to pick it up (over the side of the bluff).

BEDDING RIDGE

You can sometimes see ridges on aerial photos if you focus on the shadowing that was in place at the time the photo was taken, but normally you will need a topo map where these terrain features jump out easily. Look for stacked curves or ovals. The farther the lines are apart, the flatter the ridge. Often, ridges will be quite flat at the top but steep on the sides. The flat top is signified by the width of the innermost oval or curving contour line. Ridges don't need to be wide to serve as bedding areas.

Deer love bedding on all ridges because they can position themselves where they smell everything behind them and see everything below — in front of them. Because they love to bed in these places, ridges are potential stand locations during the rut when bucks are actively seeking does.

I love to hunt wooded ridges in the morning during the rut. Does bed there consistently, and the bucks come looking for them shortly after sunrise. If the ridge has a number of knobs and points — all of which represent features within the feature that will affect deer movement — I could spend the whole season hunting just one ridge top and the rest of this chapter telling you how I would do it. However, I'll just leave the fine points for you to discover.

Generally speaking, deer will tend to bed on the downwind side of the ridge. As mentioned, this permits them to smell anything behind them and see anything in front of them. Further, they like to bed on secondary points extending from the main ridge. You can see these secondary ridges as dimples outward on the contour lines of the topo map.

Deer (bucks included) will tend to follow contour lines when traveling from one bedding point to the other. Stands located near the head of any draws leading upward toward the ridge (these are apparent because the ridge necks down in the areas of these draws) are well positioned for this type of movement. This stand location has the added benefit of permitting you to see what is happening on the ridge top while using the draw as a low-profile stand entry and exit route.

Bill Winke took this nice 10-pointer in early November 2009 while hunting from a stand on a wooded ridge. The buck was cruising through the area hunting for does when the author grunted him close enough for a shot. Bedding ridges represent great morning stands during the rut.

Chapter 7

Timing Is Everything

Bill Winke shot this nice buck in early September. The buck was headed to a feeding area in the afternoon, but Winke picked him off at a water hole between his bedding and feeding areas. Hunting deer right at their Point A or Point B is tough for a number of reasons, but finding a funnel between the two places makes the hunt much easier.

I have now given you the foundation for seeing terrain features differently – as funnels that concentrate deer movement, increasing your odds for getting a nice buck within range. Once you start to look for them, you will see terrain funnels everywhere. Now it is time to go into some detail about which funnels to hunt at various times of the season.

FIND POINT A AND POINT B FIRST

For a funnel to make any sense, it has to lie between where the deer is and where it wants to go. In other words, you need a realistic Point A and Point B. The best funnels are the ones that lie between these two points. So, our first mission in designing a strategy for any particular part of the season is to figure out where the deer are and where they are likely to go. Point A and Point B change throughout the season.

EARLY SEASON

In the early season, Point A in the evening is the bedding area and Point B is the feeding area. In the morning, it reverses. So, when hunting the early season, you can hunt either one of the two end points or a funnel between them. As I mentioned in an earlier chapter, hunting the endpoints is fraught with problems. Walking into a bedding area in the afternoon is foolish, because you can't get to the stand without educating deer. Likewise, hunting a feeding area in the evening is tough because you have to fool many deer for possibly a long time and then get away clean at the end of legal shooting time; not easy.

Reversing this is just as problematic in the mornings. It makes no sense to hunt a feeding area in the morning because the deer are already there (or are leaving), and it can be hard to get away from a bedding-area stand after the deer have settled in when hunting a bedding area in the morning.

Sure, you can make the evening feeding area work, and you can make the morning bedding area work, but it is much cleaner to hunt a funnel in between

During the evenings early in the rut, bucks will frequent feeding areas as they look for does. However, after the bucks pester the does for several days, the does will stop coming out in the open to feed. By mid-rut, the activity around the feeding areas drops off dramatically. It will pick up again after breeding is completed.

Funnels and the rut go hand in hand. In fact, there is likely no more consistent way to hunt the rut than to find a funnel, such as this creek crossing between two doe bedding areas.

the two endpoints. You can get to and from the stand easily without alerting deer, and you should get a crack at them on their feet earlier in the evening than if you sit on a food source.

Once you have determined Point A and Point B, you can often find some kind of terrain-related (or cover-related) funnel in between. Keep it simple; that should be your goal.

THE RUT

The rut is when funnels really shine. Since bucks are moving more during daylight and covering ground looking for does, they will pass through these bottlenecks regularly. Point A and Point B are still fairly well defined, but they are different from what they were during the early season.

During the rut, bucks are not as focused on feeding. Instead, they will spend more time looking for does. So, places where does concentrate tend to be the bucks' Point A and Point B. These are doe bedding areas and doe feeding areas. In the evening, a stand out on the fringe of the feeding area is a good choice, ideally in some kind of natural funnel just deep enough in the timber that you can sneak out at the end of legal shooting time without alerting the deer. This is not a lot different from where you might hunt in the early season.

Things change dramatically in the morning, however. This is because Point A and Point B both tend to be doe bedding areas. Now, you have bucks flowing through all kinds of places they might not frequent at other times of the year. For example, if does bed on two ridges separated by a ditch, the bucks are likely to travel through any areas of the ditch where the banks are gradual, forming a classic morning hunting location for the rut. At other times of the year, these spots may not see much buck movement at all.

Plot out all the doe bedding areas in your hunting area on a topo map and aerial photo. Then look for any terrain or cover features that form funnels between two of them. These are all potential stand locations during the rut. The ones you hunt should be those that set up best for undetected entry and exit and where the wind is steady, without any swirling.

LATE SEASON

The late-season patterns of bucks are very similar to their early-season patterns: bedding area to feeding area and back again. In my experience, it is very hard to hunt late-season bucks anywhere near their bedding areas. So, realistically, we are dealing with two potential strategies: hunt the feeding areas or hunt funnels between bedding areas and feeding areas. The first strategy works if the bucks are getting to their feeding areas in daylight. The second works if the distance between bedding and feeding areas is great enough that you can slip in undetected.

Again, we are looking for terrain features that serve to funnel bucks between Point A and Point B. When you simplify deer hunting down to its most fundamental parts, that is really what you should be doing every time you hang a stand. That is why recognizing what the different features look like in the field and on paper, and understanding how terrain features influence deer movement, is such an important part of deer hunting.

Bill Winke took this old buck toward the end of the 2012 season while hunting an open gate on the edge of a late-season food source. Not all funnels are produced by terrain, but having funnels near your stand will always increase your odds for success, regardless of the time of season.

Chapter 8

Focusing on Creek Funnels

Any time you can find a creek flowing through a timbered area, you have found the potential for not only an undetected entry and exit route but a deer super-highway. Deer travel the banks of creeks and cross at select spots, creating great funnels.

So far, I have gone into some detail regarding the many different kinds of terrain features you can find in the whitetail woods. I am sure I have only scratched the surface of what you will find when you start scouting and studying the maps and photos. However, at least you have the basic understanding of how deer relate to terrain so you can easily figure out how to hunt other features you run across. With all this background work, a lot of the ground has already been plowed related to creeks and ditches, but there are still some details specific to these terrain features worth exploring further. In this chapter, I will focus on creeks.

There are few things in the world of whitetail hunting you can count on to produce action every year; creeks are one of them. Everywhere I've found creeks in deer country, I have easily found excellent stand locations. If there is a creek winding through your hunting area, you have a great opportunity to enjoy the best season of your life.

I know every bend, sand bar and high bank on the many creeks that wind through my hunting areas. I've walked them dozens of times. Creeks are also the first place I start looking when hunting a new area.

Creeks should play into your strategies for two reasons. First, they funnel and influence deer movement in a very predictable way. You can take advantage of anything that's predictable. Second, as we have discussed already, they are perfect avenues for undetected access to these same locations. That's the best definition for a great stand: one that funnels deer and is easy to access without educating deer.

Such spots are no-brainers once you find them. You don't think about it anymore; you start hunting. Few places in the white-tail woods combine these elements better than creeks. Creeks have become the centerpiece of my hunting. A few seasons back, I took two bucks from creek stands, and those hunts serve as an illustration of how easy it is to set up a great ambush on a creek.

I arrowed the first buck while hunting a creek that snaked through wide-open winter wheat fields. The buck was walking along a high bank on an outside bend between two inside bends. The narrow ribbon of trees that lined the high bank was the only thing that joined the two larger patches of cover. With the rut coming, that buck was out checking the blocks of cover for does when he came right past my stand for a 15-yard shot.

The creek provided more than just a funnel, it also provided a great way to ensure no deer smelled me or saw me as I approached the stand. I had picked a big tree right next to

Author Bill Winke loves to use creeks to access his hunting area because it is easy to stay below the line of sight of nearby deer and keep scent and sound to an absolute minimum.

the steepest part of the creek bank and used chest waders to cross the creek and work my way under the bank right to the base of the tree. Using roots, I climbed to the base of the tree where I stashed the waders and put on a pair of warm boots. There was no way a deer could ever run across my ground scent near that stand, and it was unlikely any would see me or hear me approaching.

With the wind blowing my scent out over the creek, there was also no way a deer on my side could ever smell me. Even though I shot the buck on the first morning I hunted the stand, I'm sure I could have sat there every day that the wind cooperated without any risk of educating deer.

The second buck that season was actually using a low crossing in a creek when I tagged him. The creek ran through a large area of timber, so there was plenty of cover. The crossing itself was the funnel that brought the buck within 22 yards. Again, the creek served as a low-profile access

Bill Winke shot this buck along the high bank of a creek that flowed through a winter wheat field. Winke used waders to cross the creek and slip right to the high bank under his treestand before slipping into hunting boots and scaling the tree. The strategy produced an easy, 15-yard shot.

route that I used to reach the stand without being seen or heard, but its primary purpose was to funnel deer traffic.

TRAVEL FUNNELS

Deer don't like to swim when they can walk across a stream or river, and they don't like to climb up and down steep banks if a short detour will bring them to a gradual slope. This is why shallow-water crossings are some of the very best natural deer funnels, and they usually occur, for reasons I will discuss soon, in the areas where you find gradual banks. This makes for a funnel that is very easy to find and hunt.

Deer also form trail systems that run along the banks of a stream, producing a second travel route to consider when deciding on a stand location near a crossing. Creeks that are isolated in otherwise open terrain have a significant advantage in this regard. The deer are much more likely to use the thin strip of cover along high banks when traveling from one patch of cover (one inside bend) to the other. The

Creeks provide more than just great funnels; they also provide a means to get to and from stands without being detected by nearby deer. Using creeks as your starting point is the one of the best strategies you can use when setting up stand locations.

deeper the water or steeper the bank, the less likely deer are to cross the creek. Any outside bend becomes a potential funnel. When the water is low and the bank is gradual, deer use the creek crossings between bends more heavily so these outside bends aren't as productive in that setting.

CREEKS IN OPEN COUNTRY

A creek in open country is different from a creek that runs through a large block of timber. An open-country creek is not only the dominant terrain feature but also the dominant cover feature. Think of a creek as a series of attached S curves. In open country, the cover is usually on the inside bend of each loop of the S. Pull out an aerial photo of most of Nebraska, Kansas, eastern Colorado, South and North Dakota and west-central Iowa and you'll immediately see what I mean. The inside bends have all the cover.

Here is how the bucks relate to that cover. Bucks traveling along a creek looking for does are likely to cross at the middle of an S bend (where the bank is nearly always most gradual) going from the corner of one block of cover on the creek to the next. Visualize this: they are actually crossing the creek or shallow river from the corner of the cover on one side to the opposite corner of the cover on the other side. You will find great trails in these places. Just look for the middle of the S-curve (midway between the bends) and you can't go wrong. These corners just also happen to be the places where deer often enter the feeding areas on the inside bends, as well. These are obviously great stand locations for both reasons.

However, in areas where the creek banks are too steep or the water too deep to permit an easy crossing at the middle of the S-curve, the bucks will essentially stay on their side of the creek (or river) and go around the outside of the adjacent bend to the inside of the next bend. In agricultural country, there is usually just a narrow strip of trees along this outside bend, making it a good funnel location.

So, the nature of the creek or river itself will tell you which of these two locations offers the best opportunity for traveling bucks. If there are high banks and deep water, focus on the outside bends. But if you have lower water crossings and banks that are more gradual, focus on the crossings midway between the bends.

Other open-country creek patterns: Forget about bucks traveling from bend to bend for a minute. A rutting buck along a creek that cuts through open country is vulnerable in the mornings back in the deepest cover of an inside bend (near the creek or river where does usually bed) and vulnerable again near the agricultural feeding area that nearly always lies inside these bends. You can hunt the morning stand by wading across the creek in the pre-dawn dark and getting in there before the deer. I have done this many times and it is a killer strategy. I have even stashed small boats and floated across in order to get to these spots undetected. When you hunt with the wind coming from the cover toward the creek or river, your setup is nearly undetectable.

You can hunt the afternoons by coming straight at the outside bend of the creek and then working carefully around the bend until you come to the first good trail entering the feeding area from the cover of the inside bend. That keeps you from bumping into the deer that are bedding on the inside bend.

I realize this is a bit complex to follow, but take a little time and study through this a few times. I've spent dozens of weeks hunting creeks and rivers in wide-open wheat, pasture and alfalfa country. If you do it right, you can have

Bill Winke took this massive buck with a 22-yard shot from a stand at a crossing on creek that ran through a big block of timber. It was late November, the second peak of the season's rut, and the buck was out cruising. Creeks produce great stand sites whether in open country or in timbered areas.

Deer form heavy travel routes along creeks, and this is even more pronounced in areas where the banks are too steep for the deer to cross. When setting up on creeks, be sure to understand all the ways deer relate to this important terrain feature.

great success. But if you do it wrong, every deer in these thin strips of cover will know you are there and you will have some long, miserable days in the stand.

CREEKS IN TIMBERED VALLEYS

Some creek crossings may look great but hunting them is futile. These are found where creeks wind through ravines and narrow valleys. The sign can be fabulous, but its lure is the siren song of deer hunting — like the flame to a moth. It sucks you in and then kills you!

The problem with these great-looking spots is the wind. It swirls through these places like eddies in a flood-swollen trout stream. It's impossible to sit in such a stand for long without polluting the entire lowland area with human scent.

Whenever you have an area that is protected from the direct flow of the wind, you will have swirling in that area. It can be a narrow valley and it can even be the backside of a line of thick trees. The wind swirls into these protected pockets of air and takes your scent in all directions. If the wind gusts, the swirling is even more pronounced.

As you can see, the steadiest winds will always be in areas with light cover close to either flat ground or on the tops of ridges. Anytime you change that formula toward thick cover and protected hollows, you will have to deal with swirling. It is one of the harsh realities of deer hunting. So, this is where we find ourselves, unfortunately. As relates to creeks flowing through valleys and ravines, the sign is awesome, the funnels are there and the access in and out is top notch (walking in the creek), but the wind swirls unmercifully. The result is a challenging setup, at best.

Regardless of how good a creek crossing looks, if it is located out of the direct flow of the wind, the swirling that occurs will educate every deer within hundreds of yards.

There are only three situations when it makes sense to hunt such a spot. The first one is right at the end of your hunting vacation when you have nothing to lose and the possibility of educating the deer is not as damaging. Then I say it is time to give it a try. Don't be tempted to hunt this spot too early in the hunt, though.

The second exception occurs when the wind is very low and blowing in the direction of the valley. You will at least have a safe area (upwind) where deer can't smell you. Sure, you will be giving away everything downwind, which can be a real problem if deer can possibly come from that direction, but it is better than polluting both directions. Of course, you have to have the right setup for this, with your stand being on the downwind side of the crossing and possibly even just upwind of a big bend in the creek that will keep many deer from getting on your downwind side.

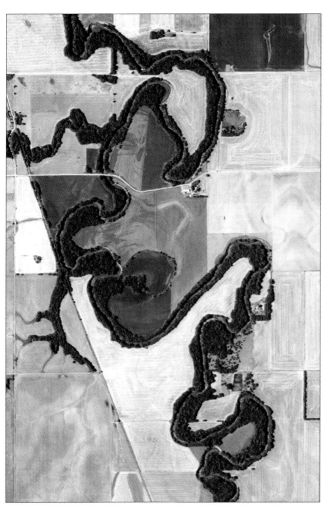

The third opportunity for hunting these valley crossings is probably the best. If the winds die right off to nothing, thermal air currents will kick in. As the air cools down shortly after the valley falls into shadow, this heavy, cooler air will descend. It will pull your scent slowly to the ground, and then take it along the ground as it flows downhill. Cold-air thermals (normally early in the morning and again toward evening) will

This is an area in Kansas where Bill Winke used to hunt often. You can see the classic terrain and land-use practice where the cover is on the inside of each bend. The straight stretches of this small river, between the bends, is where the bucks crossed most often from cover to cover when cruising during the rut.

Deer don't like to traverse the sheer edge of a cut bank, as seen behind this hunter. That leads them to make very well-defined funnels — crossings — where the banks are more gradual nearby.

Bill Winke killed this nice 8-pointer while hunting near a creek crossing a timbered valley. He timed the hunt to coincide with a day when the winds were very still so that thermals pulled his scent away from the crossing.

travel like slow-moving water along the terrain. In other words, if you are hunting next to the creek, your scent will follow the creek itself as it slowly eases down the valley. Once again, you need to be set up right (with your stand downstream of the crossing) to take advantage of this opportunity.

STILL-HUNTING CREEKS

Several years ago, a friend of mine opened my eyes to one of the deadliest hunting strategies I've ever seen. Randy took a big 8-pointer with his muzzleloader during the late season by sneaking low along the bottom of a frozen creek bed and then peeking over the bank at regular intervals to see what was in the fields nearby. He spotted the buck feeding in a small, isolated cornfield and crawled partially out of the creek to make the 80-yard shot.

Ditches that flow only during, and right after, rainstorms are also great for this sort of underground still-hunting. Obviously, you can do this anytime, but if you are splashing through the water, it will be hard to sneak up on anything. Take your time and move slowly and carefully and you will be amazed by how effective and deadly this strategy is.

HOW TO FIND THE BEST CROSSINGS

I have covered much of this already, but just to be thorough I will offer a few tips on how to find the best crossings from just a quick study of aerial photos and topo maps.

The biggest challenge you will face when hunting creeks that run through wooded valleys is the swirling winds that always plague such topography.

You can easily find creek crossings on a topo map or aerial photo simply by looking at the shape of the drainage. Where the creek makes an S-curve, you can be pretty sure you will find a crossing in the middle of the S, between the two high banks. When the creek makes a tight turn, you will find high banks on the outside of the turn. This serves as a funnel in its own right, as the deer follow this edge, but the high bank also promotes a funnel at the location where the banks are more gradual nearby.

When you are studying maps, the S-curve with the tightest turns will likely produce the best funnels. Gradual curves in the creek will not create as much erosion effect, and thus the banks will be lower and the quality of the funnels created by such a creek won't be as good.

Long, straight stretches of creek are typically less "hunter friendly" because the deer can cross at any point. Without funnels to concentrate movement,

You can see a number of S-bends in the creek displayed on this aerial photo. The easiest way to find a creek crossing is to start looking at the center of an S bend – the straight stretch of creek between two sharp bends.

creeks serve as little more than convenient low-impact entry and exit routes. From that standpoint, they are still very valuable, but they don't represent great stand sites that you will find when the creek snakes its way through the area, creating the high banks needed to form great crossings nearby.

I hope I have convinced you that creeks are awesome and given you a few ideas that will help you hunt them more effectively this fall. As I have said many times, my entire hunting strategy each year revolves around creeks and ditches, either for low-profile entry and exit or for the funnels they produce. Next, I will offer more detail about hunting ditches.

Chapter 9

The Easiest Stand to Find and Hunt

Bill Winke has reported on hundreds of giant bucks killed over the years. In most cases, the hunters were not aware the deer existed the day they shot it. They were just out deer hunting, sitting over a high-odds location when the buck came past. This is the way most people hunt, so having a simple strategy that works for this kind of hunting is important.

S ince I started writing 22 years ago, I've reported on a lot of huge bucks taken by hunters. The number of hunters who killed those bucks on purpose after patterning the deer and then setting up a stand based on that pattern has been very low – well under 20 percent. Most often, the hunter never knew the deer existed until it came slipping past his or her treestand. Or at best, he had seen it once during the summer, or received reports from local farmers. In no way could you say that these deer were "patterned."

Even more amazing is the number of these giant deer that were the hunter's first, or the hunter's first with a bow. It has gotten to the point where I don't even ask, because I know my heart can't bear the answer. "Yep, I just bought the bow last month. This bowhunting is really great, isn't it?" Umm, yeah sure, real great.

Most of the biggest bucks are tagged by chance, not by design. When you set out to kill one particular deer, you're taking on the master at his own game. Yes, trail cameras have allowed us to even the playing field a little more, but it is still a tough challenge. That is a game few of us will win, at least not very often. Patterning is the ultimate challenge, but there has to be a way that hunters with limited time can still take mature bucks with some level of consistency without having to run a ton of cameras and trying to pattern individual bucks. That is what this chapter is all about. Ditches represent that easy stand that nearly always produces during a season of careful hunting.

THE EASIEST STAND

It's easy to lose faith in a game plan when it starts to sound like a page from a pro football playbook. Deer behavior isn't predictable enough that we can reduce our strategy to a set of steps — a recipe. Let's face it; there are a lot of variables and moving parts in any successful hunt. There's a lot of luck involved, and a lot of

Simplicity is at the heart of genius. Deer go around ditches – that is easy to understand and easy to put into practice. Whenever you find a ditch in your hunting area, you have found at least one potential stand site.

Bill Winke shot this old buck at the head of a ditch that separated two feeding areas. It was Nov. 5, and the buck was cruising from one feeding area to the other looking for a hot doe.

stand time. The best we can do is focus on tendencies, play the odds with our stand choices and then put in the time. Simple solutions are easy to understand and trust; they produce confidence and confidence leads to more focused stand time. So, in this chapter I am going to attempt to simplify what can seem like a snarled mess.

Of all the stand locations I've hunted through the years, one setup is by far the easiest to find and hunt. It's a great spot anyone can, and should, hunt effectively. Success revolves around erosion ditches. You can find them nearly everywhere and they influence deer movement in a very predictable way. Focusing on ditches, you can completely change the way you hunt and add a new level of simplicity and clarity to your strategies.

You can walk into an area you've never seen before and within half a day be hunting some of the best stand sites on the property. Ditches are consistent producers because deer avoid them. It is like when hunting creeks: once you know where a deer won't go, you can easily find a funnel nearby. Try to pattern bucks all you want, but when it comes down to simple strategies for tagging them, I'll take the terrain, and more specifically, ditches, wherever I find them.

Here's a typical ditch layout. The ditch starts at the top of a slope as a dip or low spot in a ridge-top field. It is just enough to concentrate runoff water. As the dip rolls off down the slope, it becomes deeper and narrower; an erosion ditch forms at the bottom. Near the top of the ridge, the ditch is fairly shallow, but as it progresses, it gathers more water and by the time it hits the valley below, it is often a very impressive ravine.

Deer that are moving naturally will avoid crossing a deep ditch because there are usually easier routes nearby. That is how this very predictable funnel is created.

The steeper and deeper a ditch is, the more it acts as a deterrent to deer travel and the better job it serves to funnel that movement to areas where the banks are more gradual. Deep, steep-sided ditches are the best for funneling deer.

The deeper and steeper the banks, the better the ditch will act as a deterrent to deer movement and the better the funnels will be formed wherever the crossing is gradual — or at the very top. Similarly, ditches that have long stretches between crossings are also better because the deer movement is more concentrated at the places where the deer can cross.

FINDING THE BEST DITCHES

You don't even have to know where a deer is going or where he's coming from to hunt ditches effectively. You only need to know that there are deer in the area. Given any reason at all to travel (such as the rut or normal feeding patterns), they will use these funnels whenever they lie between a believable Point A and Point B. I wrote a whole chapter on finding Point A and Point B, so you should have a good feel for that. Any ditch that lies between these endpoints is a good candidate for a stand location.

This really simplifies the scouting process. You don't need to walk an entire piece of ground to identify potential ditch funnels. All it takes is an aerial photo and topo map and a few short hikes to check out the ditches that occur in the bottoms of obvious draws.

Topo maps do a better job of revealing ditches than aerial photos because they show the actual contour lines. You'll see a parallel zigzag in the lines in places where draws (valleys or ravines) occur. It will look like a finger pointing up toward the ridge top.

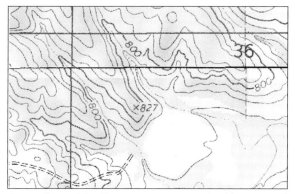

Intermittent blue lines on a topo map signify seasonal water flow, also known as runoff. When you find seasonal waterways in agricultural country, you nearly always find erosion and the ditches it creates.

In the absence of a topo map, an aerial photo will show shading, depending on the sun angle at the time the photo was taken. The shading reveals the deepest ravines, which usually have ditches at their bottoms. You still need to do a bit of foot work to be sure ditches actually exist in these areas, but in mostly agricultural areas with plenty of topsoil, these erosion ditches are nearly a given. In rocky country, they are not as predictable. The runoff will occur, but it may not produce the kind of deep, steep ditches required to funnel deer.

You can find ditches very fast by making a quick pass along a sidehill. Even areas with only moderate changes in relief can still produce ditches deep enough to funnel deer movement. As little as 50-100 feet of elevation change can produce a suitable ditch if the soil is free of shallow bedrock.

Aerial photos often show shading so you can identify valleys. In areas with ample topsoil, the existence of valleys and draws provides some assurance you will find a ditch at the bottom. These ditches are caused by erosion, so in areas with rocky soil, they are not as pronounced.

SETTING THE PERFECT AMBUSH

Walk the length of each ditch in your hunting area. You should find sections where the banks are steep and sections where they're gradual. Focus most of your attention on the ditches that are steepest and deepest. Note the places where deer cross them. Ideally, there won't be very many crossings. Each one is a potential stand site.

Now you have to decide which crossings to hunt. First, examine the landscape to figure out how the wind will flow. Without getting into this discussion again (I covered it thoroughly in the last chapter), the wind will typically swirl anytime it blows past a protected area or dead pocket of air. Anytime you hunt an area with swirling winds you are taking a big chance of burning out your hunting area. You may get lucky and tag a nice buck when the wind is just right (I've gotten away with it a few times). But more likely you will get busted by everything in the area, because your scent is washing in every direction.

If you plan to hunt an area more than once, you have to avoid situations where you can't control your scent. Taking it a step further, you need to avoid hunting areas that are protected from the direct flow of the wind. That doesn't leave a lot with respect to ditches that run along the bottoms of ravines. The ravines themselves will promote swirling. For the most part, you have one very good option — the upper end of the ditch.

As you walk up the hill along the ditch, the last good crossing closest to the top (sometimes the top itself, where deer go around the end) will offer the most consistent wind. Overwhelmingly, this is the best choice for your stand.

You have two wind options here. In one scenario, the wind will be coming over the ridge top toward the slope below you. This will presumably carry your scent over the ditch toward the valley below, although local terrain may not allow that to work. Second, the wind can be coming from the opposite direction – blowing toward the top of the ridge. I like this wind best. It takes my scent away from where I expect the deer to come from. On the best crossings, set up two stands – one above and one below the crossing – so you can hunt the spot on either of these two acceptable winds.

Normally you will find the best stand site along an entire ditch at the very head, where the ditch starts. This spot is closest to the top of the slope and therefore generally has the steadiest winds. Deer also use this funnel very consistently.

When the stand is located at the head of the ditch, the wind can be coming from the top of the ridge toward the ditch or from the ditch out across the top of the ridge. As long as you hunt the stand on the downwind side of the funnel, both setups will work.

NO-BRAINER ACCESS

Not only do deer react to deep ditches in a very predictable way, this strategy also has a second advantage. Getting to the stand without alerting deer is easy. You start at the bottom of the valley and just walk right up the ditch. Ditches are usually littered with deadfalls, so you will probably have to go in during the off-season with a chainsaw and clear a path in each of the ditches you hunt.

Using the bottom of the ditch as your entry and exit route makes great sense for three reasons: sight, sound and scent. By walking up the ditch, you stay out of sight, keep your ground scent in a place where approaching deer won't hit it and you reduce noise. This is, by definition, the perfect entry and exit scenario.

TIMING

Ditch stands can be productive at any time of the day, but it has been my experience that mornings are best. I think it has to do with buck traffic between bedding areas, which always seems to be more prevalent in the morning. Don't give up too early, though. During the rut, this kind of movement can occur right up to midday and even beyond. However, I've noticed that ditch stands are often fairly dead during the later afternoon as it seems bucks are following does toward feeding areas and are less likely to be traveling from bedding area to bedding area.

This doesn't mean a ditch stand won't produce during the afternoon, but it is just a slower time. If you don't have any better choices, there is no reason not to sit

Use a chainsaw to clear out all the ditches in your hunting area and it will be much easier to slip through them quietly and quickly when accessing your stands.

the ditch stand in the afternoon. You're not hunting the whole herd. It only takes one buck to turn your entire season into a successful one, and he can come past at any time.

If you haven't figured it out yet, I love ditches even more than I love creeks. While creeks offer some good stand locations, they are even more ideal as low-impact entry and exit routes. Ditches almost always offer one killer stand set up (the top of the ditch) as well as serving as a network of low-profile entry and exit routes for a particular property. On my farm, I have several ditches that start near the county road and dump off into the bigger ravines below. I don't hunt the top of these ditches because they are just too close to the road to afford the deer security, but I do use them extensively to sneak in and out of the property when accessing other stands deeper in the cover.

So, once again, if you aren't using ditches both for the easy and foolproof stand locations they offer and for the undetected access you can find along their bottoms, you are missing out on a great opportunity to both improve and simplify your hunting.

Chapter 10

The Terrain
10 Commandments

Sam Soholt proudly poses with a dandy buck he shot on a creek crossing. Creeks and ditches are fundamental to many good strategies when hunting broken terrain. If you want to wear a big smile like Sam's at the end of this season, learn to master these two important elements of the terrain.

This book started on the subject of entry and exit routes, took a turn through the world of funnels, then into a more detailed discussion of how the terrain forms funnels that influence deer movement. After that, we hit the stretch run as we applied all of this fundamental learning on the subject of creeks and ditches: how to find them and how to hunt them. It is no coincidence the book took that route. Your entry and exit routes are the most important thing to consider anytime you are searching for exceptional stand sites; preserving your element of surprise is critical. On top of that, knowing how to identify and hunt funnels is a critical deer-hunting skill. Finally, being able to apply these fundamentals to two very common terrain features brings it all together.

I addressed these subjects both here in the book and within the companion DVD that my staff created to make these principles of successful deer hunting even easier to understand.

Through it all, I hope you learned the following 10 key fundamentals of hunting the terrain, specifically as they relate to hunting creeks and ditches:

1. Entry and Exit: The routes you take to and from your stands are the keys to success. Creeks and ditches offer the best in low-impact entry and exit. You can keep below the sight line of most of the deer, keep your scent in places the deer don't often walk and the sound of your passing will be muffled by the closed-in nature of the banks.

2. DIY entry and exit routes: When creeks and ditches aren't available, you can improve your low-profile entry and exit by enhancing or manipulating native cover or even planting screens that will give you something to sneak behind.

3. Funnels are the key: Deer hunting and funnels go hand in hand. When you focus on your hunting area with an eye toward finding all the funnels, you will soon see stand locations you never thought existed, and you will start to make sense of all the seemingly random deer movement that occurs each fall.

4. Point A and Point B: For a funnel to make sense, it has to lie between a deer's Point A and Point B. If the spot is not between two believable endpoints, there is no point in hunting it. Why would the deer come past?

Funnels and deer hunting go hand in hand. Anything that concentrates deer movement, such as the edge of a large pond, is an ideal place for a stand.

Bedding areas used heavily by does are definitely a point of attraction for bucks during the rut. Any funnel between two such places will see action.

5. Point A and Point B change with the season: Early in the season, Point A and Point B are feeding areas and bedding areas. During the rut, Point A and Point B (for a buck) are the places where does concentrate — namely their bedding and feeding areas. During the late season, Point A and Point B are once again feeding and bedding areas.

6. Terrain produces funnels: Features of the terrain create funnels that deer relate to in a very consistent manner. Any time the landscape is broken by ridges and valleys, there will be plenty of terrain features to help you predict how deer will move. This is one of the true keys to consistent, long-term, deer-hunting success, especially when it comes to bucks. Funnels can be subtle or they can be obvious, but they will be there.

7. Creek funnels are easy to find and hunt: Creeks form two classic funnels: crossings and parallel trails that follow the banks. In different situations, these can both be killer stand sites.

8. Look for tight turns: When studying aerial photos and topo maps of creeks, focus on the tight turns. The banks will usually be high on the outside of these bends, which means that the deer will avoid crossing in that area, choosing instead to cross where the banks are more gradual. This makes a very easy funnel to find and hunt. However, sometimes when the creek winds through a valley, swirling winds will make it very hard to hunt without educating deer.

9. Ditches are serious deer funnels: In many areas, ditches that form in the bottoms of draws and ravines are steep and deep, and deer don't cross them except at locations where their banks are gradual. This makes ditches great funnel areas in broken topography.

Any time you hunt broken terrain, you will find funnels that will improve your odds for success if you just know what to look for.

10. Hunt the upper ends of ditches: Usually, the top of a ditch represents the best stand location along its entire length. It is here that the wind will be steadiest. Swirling winds that occur down in a ravine are very hard to predict. The best way to handle them is to avoid them. Focus on ditch funnels as close to the top of the ridge as possible.

If you do nothing more than master the strategies involved with hunting creeks and ditches, you will have put in place a major piece of knowledge that will lead to a lifetime of consistent success.